Discount Diva's 30 Tips to Having the Best for Less:

A Guide to Financial Freedom

Lynesha McElveen

DEDICATION

To my wonderful husband Rodney whose
unconditional love,

constant encouragement,

and relentless nudges to step out of my comfort zone
made this book possible.

I love you so much!

CONTENTS

ACKNOWLEDGMENTS

My deepest appreciation goes to 1106 Design and especially to Ronda Rawlins for my editing. Ronda you were extremely professional and patient with my numerous questions about the process. You were attentive and did you best to ensure I was completely satisfied with my product.

Thank you to fiverr.com for all the options you have in helping self-publishers cut costs. A special thanks in particular to Ilian Georgiev for my cover. You were very responsive and continued to work with me until my vision came to pass.

I can't forget Dasia Webster who proofread my book and got it back to me in record time. I also appreciate your unwavering support not only in writing this book, but in achieving all of my dreams with Liberty Educational Group and Di$count Diva.

A special thank you to Stephanie Peay who has been a constant support in both my business and personal life. Stephanie you have gone above and beyond and I appreciate you always being there to lend a helping hand.

I can't forget my friends like Tameka Williamson who took numerous phone calls and meetings about how to publish my book and never complained. Tammy Perry who continuously promotes me by sending me information about business opportunities, self-development, and things I need to know. Norise Greene for being a continuous support through both verbal communication and silent prayers. Marreon Haskell for listening to me talk for hours on end not only about my desire to write a book, but all the things I have desire and never complaining. Can't wait until we write ours together! My gratitude goes as well to the many friends who similarly encouraged me, even when they may not have even known it.

Thank you to Saideh Browne who let me know writing a book wasn't brain surgery and gave me the added push I needed and the knowledge of great vehicles like CreateSpace to get my work out there.

The biggest thanks go out to the many family members who encouraged me to undertake this project, even when I felt overwhelmed. To my mother, Beverly Reeves who dared me to dream, my mother-in-law, Betty Dorsey who believed in my dreams and my wonderful husband, Rodney McElveen who constantly spoke life into my dreams. I love you Rodney! You are my number one fan, and I am yours!

Lynesha McElveen

.

1 CHAPTER
INTRODUCTION

Why Being a Di$count Diva Is Attractive

I think becoming a Di$count Diva was just my destiny. Even as a young child I went to thrift stores with my mother, which I thought was disgusting, but I was exposed to it whether I wanted to be or not! In college, I remember watching Ricki Lake and seeing this girl show off her fabulous boots she had purchased from a thrift store in Atlanta and that's when I was sold! I knew then if I could find ways to get great stuff for less, I was all for that.

I even remember finding ways to create things in high school. For example, I used to cut off the tags from the back of my old Keds to put on the back of the new, cheap, knockoff version just to look cool. Now, I'm not a knockoff girl at all, but I learned early how to make it work with what I have. I would often try to make dresses shorter or reinvent outfits by changing them with different accessories because I didn't have a mother who was just constantly buying me the latest trends. We were by no means dirt poor, but I knew I was a clotheshorse and I always wanted newer, different, unique pieces, and in order to get them I had to be creative and innovative.

My father is credited with teaching me the "Rule of 72" when I was about 12 years old, but at the time I didn't truly understand the rule's significance. The "Rule of 72", which later in life I found to be Albert Einstein's greatest discovery tells you how long it will take for your money to double using compound interest.

As I went off to college, I began to learn about stocks, the importance of saving, and how interest really worked. I knew at that point I needed to find a way to make all things work together. The shopping and the savings, the dream home and car with the dream life, knowing how to enjoy the here-and-now while leaving an inheritance to my children's children.

Attending graduate school at the University of Cincinnati further enhanced my desire to not only learn how to be The Di$count Diva, but to teach others to do the same. I watched a city erupt into violence by people who felt discriminated against and in retaliation rioted, looted, and destroyed the city's financial gains. I was saddened by the desecration of a city that many called home and I wanted to do something to help.

I remember thinking to myself, "You don't change a system by looting and tearing things up. You change a system by leveraging your buying power." When people spend their money differently, the world pays attention.

That experience in Cincinnati became the driving force for me to teach financial literacy to anyone who would listen so I could change not just my life, but those around me!

For me, being a Di$count Diva is being able to "Have the Best for Less" and teaching others to do the same. I believe in being able to look good and still have money in the bank, drive where I want, and live where I please, but not at the expense of saving for my retirement. I believe in getting the same designer handbag as you do, but for a lot less. Being the Di$count Diva allows me to live the life I want without going broke, by saving and investing the difference I would have paid for an item and purchasing an appreciable asset.

I have spent the greater part of my life feeling that I shouldn't have to sacrifice what I want to get what I need. Why do I have to choose whether I want to pay for my children's educations or fund my retirement? Why do I have to choose whether I want to save for a home or go on a vacation? Why do I have to choose between paying off my debt or saving for my future? Well, I decided I didn't have to choose and you shouldn't have to choose either. I decided to have the best because I can! I decided to be The Di$count Diva!

I know we live in a world where delayed gratification is a foreign concept, and telling someone to live below their means is almost insulting. Our world is one where better just won't cut it and only the best will do! This is where I come in. I'm here to tell you, you CAN have the best, but a key to this concept is learning how to get your "Best" for a lot less.

The purpose of this book is to teach you my Di$count Diva tips and strategies on how to "Have the Best for Less" while creating financial freedom just by changing some of your habits, educating yourself, and being willing to explore non-traditional means for getting what you want and need.

This book is divided into several categories to help you understand how to Have the Best for Less and make your money work for you through *Saving, Investing, Cutting Expenses, Eliminating Debt and Responsible Credit Use, Savvy Shopping, Accumulating Assets, Protecting Assets, Giving, and Getting R.E.A.L.™* with yourself in the process.

2 CHAPTER
SAVING

Di$count Diva Tip #1-- Saving $1 a Day

This is the easiest way to get started with saving. If you are one of those people who think it's so hard to save, start small and start simple. Just save $1 a day. Whether you put it under your mattress, in your piggy bank, or at your local bank, take a dollar out of your wallet and save it each day. Saving $1 a day will net you $365 a year and $365 is more than $0.

If you don't want the pain of actually taking a dollar a day to the bank, then subtract $30 or $31 dollars from your account monthly to put into your savings account. I say $1 a day, because some people will look at $30 and think that it is a lot, or they start out with the intention to do it, and then life happens. If you break it down into small increments, then there is no excuse why you can't achieve it.

I mean, really, Diva's $1 a day is like not visiting the snack machine at work, or not stopping to get a pack of gum. One dollar won't even buy you a gallon of gas, so I know you can save it.

Saving $1 a day will get you in the habit of saving. It's important to develop the habit first and then you can begin saving larger amounts of money. If I came to you and told you to save 10% of your income and you make $4,000 a month and you don't save anything, then saving $400 a month will sound totally unreasonable and you will probably become overwhelmed, but if I tell you to just save $1 a day, that's something you can easily grasp and put into action.

If you are saying to yourself, "Di$count Diva, I don't even have $1 a day to save," then there will be other tips in the book that tell you how you can get that dollar. If you are stretched to the limit, then it's important to find a way to get yourself "unstretched" so you can begin building your savings.

The whole point is to help you see it is possible to save! The whole point of saving $1 a day is to give you a quick high. Once you complete a week of saving $1 a day and have $7, you will have a small sense of satisfaction. And once you complete a month of saving $1 a day, then you will know it is possible, even if you have to start with relatively small amounts.

It's not where you start Divas, it's where you finish. So start by saving $1 today!

Di$count Diva Tip #2: -- Pay Yourself First

I know this sounds simple, but many people have it in their mind to save, yet after paying all their bills they find there is nothing left. If you pay yourself first, you force yourself to adjust your spending habits so you can meet the rest of your obligations. Once you get in the habit, you won't even miss the money!

So you may ask, "How Do I Pay Myself First?" Paying Yourself First is not a unique concept; it is, however, a unique decision. It is a decision that you matter. Decide that you are just as important as everybody else. Decide that you work hard and you don't do it *just* to pay bills, but also to afford some of the things you want, like a home, vacations, retirement, or even a nice wristwatch or pair of shoes. Decide if YOU don't get paid, nobody gets paid. Decide that you love yourself enough to put yourself first.

Once you make that decision, the next part is doing it. If you have a particular time you sit down and pay your bills, include yourself as a "bill." You can title the money you pay to yourself something catchy and funny like the "I Love Me" fund, the "Me First" fund, or "My Future." Then pay that bill first, so it should look like this:

- Me First fund $400
- Mortgage $1,000
- Electric $120
- Water $25
- Car Payment $320

And so on and so forth but the point is, YOU should be first!

You should also sign up at work to participate in your company's 401K, 403B, or other retirement plan. With any of these plans, the money is taken from your paycheck before you even get it. This way is seamless because you can't spend what you don't see. Another benefit of contributing to your company retirement plan is that by doing so, you lower your taxable income. For example, if you make $4,000 a month, and you contribute 10% , or $400, to your retirement, then that makes your taxable income for the month only $3,600. This means you will only pay taxes on $3,600 vs. $4,000. As a result, many people who contribute to their company retirement plans see this as a value because they pay less in taxes.

Remember, the key to being successful is to come up with an amount that is suitable for you. Don't make the amount too high because you will likely dip back into it and thus defeat the purpose. Don't make it too low because it's for you…your **goals**…your **future**… your **dreams**, and don't you deserve the best?

You should shoot for Paying Yourself 10%, but if this feels like too much, then start with 3% and gradually work your way up. It's OK to ease into this, especially if you've never consistently saved and are not accustomed to making yourself a priority. In a year or so you may feel more comfortable with Paying Yourself 8% or you may even be ready to take on the 10%.

With the amount of bills many of us have, unexpected expenses that pop up, and impulsive shopping we sometimes do, it is important to establish the habit of Paying Yourself First. It is too easy for everybody else to get paid like Mr. Gas, Ms. Lights, and Sir Cell Phone, which sometimes causes us to struggle to have anything left over for ourselves. It's just way too easy for our money to be eaten up by life, and let's face it, life happens, and if you don't care about saving for your future, trust me all the people you pay for life's wonderful necessities and luxuries definitely won't care.

You have to make yourself #1 because nobody else will, so Pay Yourself First!

Di$count Diva Tip #3 -- Start an Automatic Savings Plan

If you are trying to save money by relying solely on your preferences, this can sometimes be quite difficult. Many times we have the best of intentions, but life gets in the way. We plan to save $200 each month, but then we get a flat tire, or our child needs money to go on a school trip, or the money just slips through our fingers.

You can achieve your financial goals of saving money much easier by starting an **automatic savings plan.** By using this approach, you can have money automatically deducted in a number of ways without having to even think about it. This way you can turn your attention to other things in life and yet still build for your financial future.

For instance, you can set up your checking account to have a portion of money automatically drafted each month into a separate account. You pick the day the draft takes place as well as the amount you want drafted. Once this is done, you can set it and forget it. This is a no-brainer; just remember to subtract the amount being drafted from your check register each month, so you don't wind up with NSF or overdraft fees.

Another way to make this even easier is to have the money automatically deducted out of your payroll check. I like this method best because the money is taken out before you even get your check, and it goes back to Tip #2, "You can't miss what isn't there." Also, this can be a way to reinforce budgeting, and if you're like me, you may need a little forced discipline in this area.

Two of the great things about automatic savings plans are you also save money by not writing checks and save time by not having to go to the bank and transfer money from one account to another. There's nothing better than saving all around!

My suggestions when doing automatic savings plans is to have the money go into an account that is not too easily accessible. If you have a debit card linked to this account, it can be too tempting to swipe the card and deplete your savings. If you can go right to the bank down the street, you might swing through and get your money to buy a cute pair of shoes. The moral of the story is, if the money is too easy to get to, even if you are having it *automatically* drafted you will be more likely to *automatically* withdraw it as well.

If you stick to this plan, you can be sure to reach your savings goals and quite possibly even reach millionaire status *automatically.*

Di$count Diva Tip #4 -- Keep 50% of All Windfall Money

So you're looking forward to getting that tax refund, you have a favorite aunt who dies and leaves you a bundle, or you get a bonus on your job! What should you do? I'll tell you what you shouldn't do. You shouldn't spend all the money on bills that you already have or to get that new toy you've been wanting. Remember, this is money you weren't expecting anyway, so why would you include this in your budget?

You can't count on a family member dying in order for you to be able to take care of your financial responsibilities, and who would want that to be the only way they can get ahead?

So now let's go on to what you *should* do….you should keep at least 50% of the windfall money. It's very easy to plan how we are going to *spend* that money. This happens usually pretty quickly. We may want new clothes, vacations, or to just pay down bills, but how many of us plan how to *keep* our windfall? For this reason, we should make a commitment to save or save 50% of all lump sum money before we even start planning how we are going to spend it.

Listen here, people, I'm no Scrooge! I didn't say keep the whole 100% although that would help you fulfill your financial dreams even faster, but I'm a realist. I know that as much as people want financial freedom, they also want to enjoy life, so I am leaving you a full 50% to do whatever you want, but the other 50% *must* be kept.

Sounds easier said than done? Of course it is! Who said it would be easy? If it were easy, everybody would be doing it and we all would be financially free, but it's not easy. It's extremely difficult and it takes discipline and commitment to save and save money we may not have even been expecting. However, if you are someone who wants to become financially free, putting this tip into practice will help you get to that goal much quicker.

I believe you can, "Have It All" and I like this rule because it allows you to splurge on life's little indulgences while still building your financial future and paying your bills while paying yourself.

Di$count Diva Tip #5 -- The Envelope System Reinvented

Many years ago there was a budgeting system created to help individuals stick to spending a certain amount of money in different categories. This was called the **envelope system.** Each envelope represented a particular area, namely wants, entertainment, shopping, beauty, or eating out. In each envelope you carried a certain amount of money, and when the money was gone, that was it!

Now this was a great way of helping people not only budget for each of their categories, but also save because any money that was left couldn't be transferred into another category. For example, if you had $100/month allotted for entertainment, but you only spent $75, you've just made $25. This money could now be added to your savings, but not anywhere else.

With the invention of debit cards and the decrease in cash carriers, however, this system became all but obsolete. Nevertheless, the system has since been reinvented, and you can still benefit from the system's principles by sticking to a certain amount of money for each category and being disciplined.

If you give yourself $400/month for shopping, you will need to break it down into amounts you can easily keep up with, like $100/week in a four-week month or $80/week in a five-week month. If you are in week three and you have spent $394, then you know you only have $6 left. There is no pulling $4 from somewhere else to get a cute top on sale, Divas!

Again, this takes discipline. It's easy to swipe that debit card to get a $20 dress that is normally $50 and rationalize the purchase. It's easy to try to justify overspending by *only* $14 when we know the dress is a great deal, but it's cheating, and I know you're not a cheater. So if you feel like you can't be honest with the debit card, I say put up the debit card for a week, and give yourself a daily cash allowance. This way, when the money for the day is gone, it's gone. Any money you have left over from the day before can be rolled over, but any money left over at the end of the month should be saved/invested versus being put into a different category.

To make the envelope system successful you should also set standards on what is a reasonable percentage to spend in each category.

Di$count Diva Tip #6 -- Build an Emergency Fund

Having an emergency fund is something that is necessary to prevent financial ruin. This is especially important in today's economy where many people are experiencing downsizing, layoffs, furloughs, and buyouts. A good rule of thumb used to be to have three to six months of living expenses saved up. However, because many people who end up out of work are taking up to a year or longer to find comparable employment, today's emergency fund should have a minimum of nine months of living expenses saved up for a rainy day. For example, if your living expenses are $4,000/month, you would need to save up $36,000 to be on track.

Remember, if you do experience a change in your income, it's very important to make adjustments to your spending as soon as possible. A mistake many people make is they are used to earning $6,000 a month and now they are only earning $4,000, but they continue to spend as if they are earning $6,000. Don't do that! If your money changes, you change!

Another reason you want to have an emergency fund is for times when you have an "emergency," such as your air conditioner conks out, or you need a new transmission in your car, or you have to pay a large deductible for your health benefits. When that happens, you don't have to dig yourself into debt by putting the unexpected purchase on credit. Having an emergency fund also prevents you from living off credit cards, borrowing, or going into debt to supplement your lifestyle if your financial situation changes.

Now some of you may be thinking, "Now it's going to be impossible to save that much!" or you may saying, "Now that's gonna take forever!" Well, don't panic. Saving up nine months of expenses is not expected to happen overnight. It may take you *several* years to get this amount saved, and that's OK!

If you want to work on getting to your goal quicker, you should cut out some of your luxury expenses from your nine-month emergency budget, e.g., cable television, specialty grocery items, entertainment, etc. Just stick to the basics. How much money will it take for you to run your house if you were only paying for the basics like rent or mortgage, utilities, groceries, and debt repayment? This means you need not include your landscaper or weekly trips to the hair salon in this budget.

So to be clear, it's not *if* you will have an emergency, but *when,* so to get the most out of your emergency fund be sure to stack it with at least nine months of living expenses. Also, be sure to put the money somewhere you can get to it when you need it -- somewhere that is not very risky, but that will give you the best interest rate, like a **money market fund**. Remember, this account is not designed for you to make great returns, but for you to have funds available when you need them.

3 CHAPTER
INVESTING

Di$count Diva Tip #7-- Seek Education on Investing

Often we spend vast amounts of time getting educated for our chosen careers. We spend years in school obtaining degrees and certifications and even on continuing education credit. We spend large amounts of money investing in our tuition, textbooks, and other expenses or maybe in our tools and equipment for our trade. Just as we spend time and money investing in our profession, let's adopt that same attitude when it comes to learning about investing for our financial future.

Now, am I suggesting you should go to school and get a four-year degree in finance or an MBA? Of course not, but I am suggesting the same amount of fervor you put into investing in your professional education, you should definitely put into your personal and financial education. And even if you don't put any effort into your professional education, you should definitely put time and money into your financial education because money is something you will have to deal with for the rest of your life. It only makes sense to learn as much as you can about it!

So just how do you learn about money? Well, you can educate yourself by reading books on the subject of investing. There are a number of authors who offer all kinds of advice on making your money grow. You can also browse the various websites on money from CNBC, to Robert Kiyosaki, and Suze Orman to Lynesha McElveen. There are almost an overwhelming number of websites that you can go to and acquire information, and once you learn some of these techniques you can begin testing them out.

Other ways you can brush up on your knowledge about investing is by joining an investment club, finding a mentor, or offering to take a rich person to lunch. I can't tell you the numerous pitfalls I've avoided just by attending an investment club meeting or talking to my mentor. Some say experience is the best teacher, but I believe exposure and observation can teach you just as much!

While you're in the midst of mentors and investment clubs, you should also consider taking courses and attending conferences. There are many financial experts that offer conferences all around the world for your convenience. If you have a particular person whose financial philosophy you like, go to their website and see if they offer a workshop. The workshops may have a nominal fee, but remember all the money you've invested in other things? What's more important than investing in yourself so you can make sound investment and financial decisions? One of the biggest mistakes you can make is getting out there with a lot of ambition and a little knowledge because it's what you *think* you should do. You are more than likely to lose all your hard-earned money and then experience *will* be your teacher.

Let's just keep it simple. Learn More, Lose Less.

Di$count Diva Tip #8 -- New to Investing, Use Small Amounts

This sounds like common sense. However, many people get excited about investing, especially when it is new to them, and make the mistake of taking all their savings, large amounts, or windfall money and investing it with little knowledge or experience in the market. This is called impulsive investing, and while it's one thing to be impulsive about buying a pair of shoes, it's another thing to be impulsive about investing thousands of dollars into funds when you are experimenting.

One thing I advise when new to investing is to use small amounts of money, or money you can afford to lose. Don't make emotional decisions about money just because you see a particular stock is selling for $7 a share and it used to sell for $50, and you think of putting $5,000 into that stock. Just don't do it! It's better to invest $100 into that stock to see how it does or better yet to see how you do, because you're the one picking the stock. If you invest with a small amount and the stock goes bad and drops down to a penny stock, you won't be as devastated as if you had invested huge amounts.

When you are investing small amounts of money, you more than likely won't be able to invest with some of the larger firms. There are, however, many companies that have been created just for the average investor. Most of these will allow you to open an online account such as Ameritrade, E-Trade, Sharebuilder, and Scottrade to name a few. You can also open accounts with many of the firms that offer mutual funds for as little as $25.

Be sure to review the fees for making trades and maintaining an account so there are no surprises. These fees can get expensive, so if this is a concern, you may want to open an automatic investment account where you commit to investing a certain amount automatically each month for a smaller fee.

Remember, it's great to be excited about investing, but don't let your emotions and impulses get the best of you. To avoid making cloudy decisions, when new to investing start out with small amounts of money you can afford to lose.

Di$count Diva Tip #9 --Try Dollar Cost Averaging

Dollar-cost averaging is a simple technique that allows you to take advantage of the market's rising and falling. It is a way to ensure that you get the most for your money by investing the same amount of money on a regular basis, usually monthly. Investing fixed amounts at set intervals can be a huge benefit. When stocks go down, you can buy more, and when they go up, you buy less. This enables you to still be able to participate in the market regardless of prices, without overpaying when the market is up or missing out on deals to accumulate more when the market is down.

In other words, if you normally invest $100/month in a stock that is $25/share, you will get four shares; however, if the price drops to $20/share, you get five. This can take some of the sting out of drops in the market, knowing you are actually increasing the number of shares you own when the market is down and putting yourself in a great position for gain when the market rebounds! The theory behind dollar-cost averaging is that over time your investments will *average* out.

Another great thing about dollar-cost averaging is that it allows you to invest with relatively small amounts of money. You can open an account with many brokerage firms for as little as $25 and can set up an automatic investment plan for as little as $50/month.

An additional thing about automated dollar-cost averaging is that you are always building your portfolio. If you have the process automated, every month you will know exactly what is in your portfolio, and in many cases you can change or adjust your selections even up to the day before your scheduled investment date. For example, if you normally buy a particular stock, but want to switch to a different one for that investment period, you can. Over time, your portfolio can grow substantially, especially the longer you are consistent with investing.

Dollar-cost averaging can be a great tool for those who are new to investing or don't have the time or desire to watch the market for ups and downs. It can be a key to helping you reach your investment goals.

Di$count Diva Tip #10-- Beat the Market by Indexing

The market can be a tricky thing. Going up, it is good when you have stock in a particular company and you are seeing great returns, but that time is bad for purchasing. Going down, it is bad when your stock prices take a hit, but great for purchasing additional shares. With the uncertainty of the market, the only way to try to beat it is to invest in everything. How do you do that?..by purchasing an **index fund**.

An index fund is like an overview of the market. It allows you to take a small snapshot of the entire market and tries to match returns found in a specific market. You can find index funds for the Dow Jones and S & P 500.

Index funds also take some of the guesswork out of choosing stocks, which for some can be overwhelming and hinder them from even getting into the market. Often people wonder what stock to buy, but with thousands of stocks to choose from they become paralyzed. Investing with an index fund can eliminate some of this anxiety.

The most important benefit of using index funds is they guarantee the market average because the index fund *is* the average, so as soon as you make an investment you know you have achieved the average return. Some good ones to try are the S & P 500 Index

Fund and Vanguard's Total Stock Market Index Fund. Typically, these funds outpace the market and provide very stable, above average returns.

So take the hocus pocus out of choosing stocks and Beat the Market by Indexing!

4 CHAPTER
CUTTING EXPENSES

Di$count Diva Tip #11-- Track Your Expenses: Decrease Outgo or Increase Input

The fact of the matter is there are only two ways to build wealth. You either decrease what is going out by saving more, spending less, and finding ways to stretch your dollar; or you increase what is coming in by making more money, finding additional streams of income, or purchasing and building assets.

One of the signature factors of decreasing outgo and increasing input is by first determining where your money is going. Don't know? Then let me help you find out. Are you one of those people who get $100 out of the ATM and have not a clue what you did with it? Tracking your expenses will help.

How do you track your expenses? It's very easy. You can do it as simply as keeping a notebook with you and writing down the date, item, and amount of money you spend on an item. Now this doesn't just mean the larger purchases like $200 on groceries, but all the way down to the $0.75 you spend at the snack machine at work. At the end of the week sit down and add up the totals and categorize your expenses.

Don't want to walk around with a piece of paper and pen? There are more advanced tools for tracking as well like online programs such as, Mint.com, IOweYou.com, and BudgetOnTheWeb.com.

The great thing about this exercise is it allows you to find areas of overspending that you may not have ever considered. For instance, the $6-$10 you spend eating lunch out each day actually turns into $200-$300/month, and that's just in one category. Imagine when you sit down and look at your expenses for an entire week…or a month. You will truly get a picture of where your money is going, so if you are one of those people who always say, "I make good money, but I don't know where it is going," tracking will help you figure it out.

Once you find out where your money is going, it's up to you to decide how you will cut your expenses. You may not say you won't eat out at all, but you may cut down from eating out seven days a week to eating out only three days. Discipline is the key to both writing down all your expenses and deciding where to cut.

So, Track Your Expenses and Stack Your Chips!

Di$count Diva Tip #12-- Try a Financial Fast

Just as a fast from food can help to cleanse the body from toxic chemicals, help you lose weight, and give you spiritual clarity, a **fast** from spending can cleanse the mind from toxic spending habits, help you develop healthier money thoughts, and give clarity into why you are spending money and what purpose you are trying to achieve.

So how do you fast from spending? You can tailor it however you want. You may want to fast for two weeks from eating out and pocket the money you would normally spend, or fast from impulse buying for a period of time, or fast from use of credit. All this will enable you to truly see the impact of fasting on *all* spending that is not directly related to necessities.

For example, a total fast would mean you wouldn't spend any money eating out, shopping, and on any kind of entertainment. You can't stop for coffee in the morning, so make it at home, and you can't purchase gifts. There will be no getting your hair done or going to the nail salon. The only money you will spend would be on paying your bills, debts, and maintenance, i.e., groceries.

While this requires some discipline on your part, the amount of money you will save during the fast could be hundreds of dollars. You will be tempted to spend during this fast, just as we are tempted to eat during a fast from food, but if you push through the feelings, you will begin to discover some of the emotions that accompany your spending.

You may find out, as I did, that often you will spend when bored. Shopping was my "go to," so although I liked to shop, I found myself doing it even more when I didn't have anything else to occupy my time.

You may also find out you shop because you feel your financial goals are insurmountable. Maybe you've been saving for a house, but can't seem to get to that 3%-5% fast enough for an FHA loan or saving 20% down seems impossible, so instead of saving, you now start spending. A financial fast may help you figure out that you are spending on more easily attainable objects (a pair of shoes) to substitute getting the more difficult item that you really want (the house).

This fast will also help you curb your need to consume things. It is said that it takes 21 days to form a habit, so if you do this fast for a minimum of 21 days, you can be sure to have gained more control of your money and grown your savings in the process.

Di$count Diva Tip #13 -- Look for Di$counts in Unexpected Places

A big part of building wealth can be cutting costs. In order to do this, it is important to be creative. Look for di$counts in unexpected places. What do I mean by "unexpected places"? The di$counts could be right there at the Five Star Restaurant where you love to dine or at the Spa where you love to indulge. Don't be afraid to ask for discounts on services you already get.

So how can you save at your favorite restaurant? Ask them if they have a cocktail or happy hour menu or if they offer any di$counts between certain hours. Some restaurants significantly di$count their meals during the hours of 5:00-6:30 pm to try to get people in before the dinner rush. They may even have di$counted lunch meals or have a "Ladies Night" where you can get a meal for half price. This can save your wallet and your shape because many of these meals are smaller portions.

What about your favorite place to get a massage, facial or other beauty regimen? Ask about di$count service days. They may be on a Monday, a day when the beauty industry is traditionally closed or slow. If your personal salon doesn't offer them, check into beauty or massage schools. You may be able to get a massage for as little as $25 and some schools offer them for free.

You can sign up for websites like Living Social and Scoutmob to send deals directly to your email or your cell phone. You might be surprised at the places that offer coupons. Save on getting tickets to a play, going horseback riding, attending a sporting event, or visiting a winery. Have fun, but just do it for less!

Save money on having car maintenance done by asking for di$counts at the dealership. Surprisingly, even luxury car dealerships offer di$counts on some of their services. You never know unless you ask.

By keeping more of your money you increase your wealth, so don't forget to look for Di$counts in unexpected places!

Di$count Diva Tip #14 -- Cut Expenses by Cost Sharing

In today's economic times, it is sometimes hard to get the things we want and make ends meet. We know we must first take care of our needs, e.g., living expenses, shelter, food, and utilities. This is where **cost sharing** can come in handy. I'm not talking about sharing the expenses of a healthcare plan, but I'm talking about sharing your personal expenses with someone.

One of our most basic needs is shelter. If you're single, instead of getting a one bedroom apartment, get a two bedroom, a roommate, and split the rent. This not only applies to the rent, but the utilities as well. Why are you paying all of the utilities in the apartment you share? If you have a home with a spare room, rent out one of the rooms. Why not share some of the costs of your mortgage with someone else? You can even share the costs of yard work by starting a co-op in your neighborhood, where each person is responsible for completing a certain tasks like cutting grass, raking leaves, shoveling snow, or even picking up trash. This way you are saving because you are not spending money on these expenses.

Share the cost of the price of wireless internet with your next door neighbor. Make sure it's legal first by calling your phone company. If your internet provider says it's OK, then talk to your friendly neighbor about splitting the cost. If he/she agrees, buy a router, set up an account, and save $20 or so a month!

Maybe you're a little too private to share your space? What about sharing groceries? Like all other things, the price of groceries has gone up tremendously. One way to combat these price hikes is by cost sharing. You can do this by getting a friend or group of friends and pooling your money to buy items in bulk, then splitting the cost and items evenly.

This works especially well for single people or those with small families. You get the items you need and want without overpaying or overbuying and letting items go to waste. A great place to try this is at your local Farmer's Markets, Sam's, BJ's, Costco, or any other stores or wholesale retailers that sell items in bulk.

Keep costs under control by cost sharing with neighbors and friends!

5 CHAPTER
SAVVY SHOPPING

Di$count Diva Tip #15 -- Be S.M.A.R.T. about Spending

In today's economy more than ever, it is important to be S.M.A.R.T. about your spending. Being S.M.A.R.T. just means learning to be:

<u>S</u>avvy about Shopping by Saving Money

<u>M</u>anaging your Money

<u>A</u>ccumulating Assets and setting Achievable Goals,

<u>R</u>etiring well and purchasing Real Estate

<u>T</u>raditional Investments

So let me show you how to put these tips into action?

Savvy Shopping is finding ways to get the items you like for less. This may be shopping at discount stores, thrift stores, consignment shops, and pawn shops. Savvy shopping isn't just finding inexpensive ways to cut costs, but it's doing something with the savings to build wealth. For example, if you have $700 allotted for a new TV and you catch it on sale for $399, that doesn't mean now you get to buy a High Definition DVD player and other accessories. What it means is you now have an extra $301 to **Save** and contribute to building your emergency fund, retirement fund, or investment portfolio.

You should be **saving** a set amount that is right for you to achieve your personal goals. I recommend putting a minimum of 3% into a savings account each pay period. I also recommend you find ways to save money on your fixed costs like internet service, cell phone bills, and insurance. You can do this by switching services, getting all your policies from the same insurance company, and raising your deductible.   Be sure to save the money you cut on these costs and add it to your rainy day fund.

You should also identify the items you spend miscellaneous money on and cut costs in those areas. David Bach calls this the "Latte Factor." For example, if you purchase a cup of coffee and snack every day for $5, you are spending approximately $150 a month. If you cut this back to buying coffee and a snack only three days a week, you could easily save $100 a month, and this is just in one category. What if you identify several of your "Latte Factors," e.g., buying snacks daily from snack machines, going to the mall during your lunch hour, and eating lunch out daily? Remember, it's the small splurges we often don't realize that cost us the most money.   Once you identify these factors, cut back and save the difference.

Managing your money can be a task. You can do this the old fashioned way like using your check registry and writing down all your expenses, or developing a written budget and reviewing it on a daily or weekly basis, or you can use online software like Quik Books or Mint.com to track your expenses and send you alerts when you are nearing the end of your budget in specific areas.

Achieving goals and accumulating assets can seem like a grueling process, but if you link your goals to things that are important to you, like health, relationships, and lifestyle, it will help you stay focused on your goals. For instance, if your goal is to earn $70,000, identify how earning this money will positively impact your life. Will it allow you to put your children in a private school, or buy a home, or help care for your parents? Will it allow you to take vacations with your family and spend more quality time with loved ones?

Accumulating assets is just another way to build wealth, increase your net worth, and develop an inheritance for future generations. You must first figure out what assets you are interested in accumulating. Do you want just liquid cash, or do you want property? Do you want jewelry, art work, or a combination of them all? Do you want to start a business or buy into a franchise? All of these are questions only you can answer.

Setting aside money for **retirement** and putting money towards **real estate** are two of the most important ways to prepare for your future. We know the days of Social Security are numbered, and depending on others to take care of you in retirement is not a plan! You should be actively investing in your **401K, 403B,** or **Individual Retirement Account (IRA).** Be sure to talk with a financial planner so you know you are saving enough money to live comfortably in retirement. Be sure to pay off your home so you won't have to pay a mortgage in retirement. Also, look into purchasing additional real estate. Real estate almost always appreciates in value, and once paid for can provide a nice additional stream of income.

Traditional investments are things like **stocks, bonds,** and **mutual funds**. There are also less volatile investments like **money markets, certificates of deposits (CDs),** and **notes.** Be sure to educate yourself first when investing in the market and learn your risk tolerance, in order to minimize risks and pick stocks that are in line with your investment philosophies. When purchasing investments, be sure to plan when to switch from higher risk stocks to lower risk bonds based on your age and goals. Understanding the "Rule of 72," will also help you know how long it will take for your money to double. Remember the easiest way to understand this rule is to take the interest rate and divide it by 72. For example:

72/2% interest means your investment will double in 36 years

72/6% interest means your investment will double in 12 years

72/12% interest means your investment will double in 6 years

That means:

$1,000 if invested in a 12% interest bearing account will double to $2,000 in 6 years and that $2,000 will double to $4,000 by year 12, and that $4,000 will double to $8,000 in 18 years without ever adding another penny to it! Then of course, $8,000 becomes $16,000, then $32,000, $64,000 and so on and so forth. Now if you are adding money to the account, then that money doubles as well! The "Rule of 72" is what separates the rich from the wealthy and allows people to live off of the interest of their money without depleting their principle.

Imagine having $300,000 sitting somewhere gaining 10% interest and giving you $30,000 a year in income or $1,000,000 giving you $100,000 a year. This would happen without you losing any of the value of $300,000 or $1,000,000.

Learning to be **S.M.A.R.T.** about your spending will help you have what you want, live how yow you want, and build wealth in the process!

Di$count Diva Tip #16 -- Try Bartering

Bartering goes back to the beginning of time; however, as we've become more advanced we've gotten away from it and become more accustomed to using coin/money for purchases. Today bartering is making a comeback. You can barter on almost anything, including products, services, consulting, and time. Bartering is exchanging a good or service for another good or service without the transfer of money.

Apply this to finance by finding someone who provides some type of financial service, e.g., life coaching or accounting, and trade an hour of your time and talent for an hour of their time. Apply it to items by swapping something you don't want for something you do. For example, trade a pair of shoes for a new purse, or a coat for a suit. You can even plan parties to make this fun.

Swap/Trade parties are a way to get together with friends, have food and fun, and get new items for free. Everyone who comes to this kind of party must have an item to trade. For every item they bring to trade, they can get a "new" item for themselves. I have gotten some of my best trinkets from trade parties, including a St. John top, Gucci purse, brand new Coup D'Etat boots, and Stewart Weitzman shoes. You can even trade small household items like vases, coasters, picture frames, etc.

Another way you can use bartering is by negotiating at consignment, resale, and vintage shops. Many stores offer you the ability to trade or obtain store credit for items you sell to the store. Some good stores to try are Plato's Closet, Lucky Exchange, and Raga-a-Rama. You may also try bartering at flea markets and yard sales.

There are also a variety of ways to exchange your goods online, including tradeway.com, u-exchange.com, and barterquest.com. These sites allow you to go online and trade items without using money. Some sites charge a small transaction or membership fee, but others don't.

Bartering allows you to get something you want without having to spend any of your hard-earned money. You will then have more chips to stack.

Di$count Diva Tip #17 -- Try Couponing

OK, OK, I have to admit I am new to this, but I am finding out using **coupons** on groceries, toiletries, and household items if done consistently can tremendously cut your bills. While couponing takes some time, the savings can be well worth it if you end up getting $200 worth of groceries for $100 or even for free. Also, you can check certain websites like www.hip2save.com, www.slickdeals.net and www.dealigg.com for daily deals on EVERYTHING from groceries, to electronics, to appliances, to travel.

These sites can be somewhat overwhelming, so you may want to start with a general site, such as your local grocery store. Some good ones to try are Publix and Target. They often offer great "buy one, get one free" or (BOGO) coupons, and some of these coupons you can even use at other retailers like Wal-Mart and get items for the Wal-Mart price. For example, if there is a sale on potato chips at Publix and they are "buy one get one free" for $3, you can take that coupon to Wal-Mart that may have the same chips for $2. Now you've gotten two bags of chips for $2 or one bag each for $1. That's a good deal!

Some coupons you have to cut out of store flyers, but then there are others that come in the local newspaper. Always get the Sunday paper because they have some of the best coupons.

You can also use some additional websites that will send coupons directly to your phone. Some to try are www.ScoutMob.com and www.LivingSocial.com. With Scoutmob, you can flash your cell phone and get half price meals, discounts on beauty services, and deals on things like horseback riding and visits to wineries.

Couponing can even allow you to get certain items for free like pasta, toothpaste, eggs, and even smart phones. Couponing can be addictive so be sure that once you cut the costs, you save and invest the difference! Don't continue to buy and stockpile items just for the sake of having them or because the price was too good to resist. If you do this, you will end up spending more money than you need to and really won't be saving anything at all.

Couponing can also be time consuming, so be sure you don't trade the money you are saving for the time that you can't replace. But if you can conquer not buying things just because you have a coupon and not wasting hours on end trying to coupon, you can gain huge benefits from couponing.

Use coupons and save a bundle!

Di$count Diva Tip # 18 -- Find Innovative Ways to Get What You Want for Less

You can often find the items you want by looking for them in little known places, e.g., **thrift stores, discount stores, wholesale stores, liquidation stores,** etc. The best thing about these places is you often find unique items that you could never find at traditional stores. Shopping in these innovative ways is fun. It's like a treasure hunt because you never know exactly what you will walk out with! Below are some innovative ways to get what you want for less!

Thrift Stores

These stores are found in almost every city in the world. The items are accumulated from people who donate things they no longer want. They could be new or gently used items, or well-worn items. Some people donate antiques, artwork, and even jewelry. You can get furniture and electronics at thrift stores. Some thrift stores even get brand new merchandise from local malls.

Some of my best finds include a brand new Ralph Lauren dress shirt with a $98.00 price tag for $3.98, a $7.00 Coach Bag, a $3.00 pair of Gucci shoes that were "buy one get one free," and a $15.00 Diane Von Furstenberg dress. I've also gotten a solid wood furniture set with a table, chair, and love seat for $143.00!

The fact that thrift stores are constantly getting new items daily is also an allure. You never know what you will find from one day to the next. By the same token, this means if you find something you like, you better get it right then, because it might not be there when you return, and even if it is, you might not be able to find it!

You can find a thrift store in almost every city of the world. Some thrift stores that are nationwide include Goodwill, Salvation Army, and St. Vincent DePaul. There are of course many, many others. I even look up thrift stores before I travel to different cities, and visit websites that rank the stores so I can narrow down my choices. By thrift shopping you are sure to get the best items for the best prices as long as you aren't turned off by the search!

The regular prices at thrift stores can be extremely low, but many thrift stores even offer 50%-off days or may have different colored tags that offer 10-75% off the already low prices. Another great thing about thrift stores is some actually offer job training, computer skills, business training, and education to the public. Some even donate cars to those in need.

Thrift shopping is a great way to get some things you like and help others at the same time!

Consignment Shops

These shops typically offer higher-end, previously owned clothing. Most consignment shops only accept designer labels and clothing that is current. The clothing must also be dry cleaned and in great condition. Because the items offered at consignment shops are typically higher end, the prices are usually higher as well.

Consignment shops are a swell place to find a great suit for work, or a high-end designer bag. There are even some consignment shops that offer furniture and baby clothes.

I know a couple who make great money, yet for the first six months of their daughter's life purchased all her clothing from consignment stores, and she was the best dressed baby I had ever seen. After I had commented numerous times on how adorably she was dressed, they shared that they took all the gifts they received from the baby shower they didn't use and exchanged them at consignment shops. They continued to trade items as the baby outgrew things and got pretty much all of her items by consigning. Now this couple made six figures and was clearly able to afford buying new items, but they *chose* to buy their baby's items at consignment stores, and if they hadn't told me I *never* would have known.

Prices at consignment shops are typically set; however, some shops allow you to negotiate, as I did with my best purchase at a consignment shop… a $5,000 Derek Lam purse. The purse was marked at $165, but I asked the saleslady, "Can I get a discount?"

She remarked, "Honey, it's a $5,000 bag." I remarked, "So, can I get a discount?" and she gave it to me for $150!

Other purchases include St. John suits for $140 and a Beaver fur coat for $175 from a consignment shop that marked down their furs 75% on Black Friday.

Another benefit of consignment shopping is you can bring some of your own clothing you are no longer wearing and earn money for it. We all typically have items in our closets we don't wear. Instead of just letting them sit there and collect dust, why not consign them off? You will typically earn anywhere from 40-50% of what the item sells for. So consigning is great because it lets the Diva find great buys and make some money in the process.

Before you go out spending hundreds or thousands of dollars on designer fares, check your local consignment shop!

Di$count Stores

Most of us know about local discount stores. These can range from TJ Maxx to Marshall's to Home Goods to Loehmann's. The discounts they offer mean more money in your pocket.

Some of the items at these stores may have slight defects, but many of these items have been sent there because the store that sent them had an abundance of the same thing and needed to dispose of some of it. The type of items you get at discount stores varies by area and location. Many stores cater to their specific clientele, so you may be able to buy higher-end items at different stores in the same location.

Discount stores also have days they get new merchandise in and mark old merchandise down. Ask the specific store for details.

The best way to shop discount stores is to visit the clearance racks first. These racks will have items with markdowns on top of the already low prices. I recently purchased a dress at a discount store that had a $149.00 Suggested Retail Price, but was marked down to $9.99. I have also gotten items like Donna Karan jackets for $4.99 and Sam Edelman boots for $49.00.

A great thing about discount stores is they have items like housewares, toiletries, organizers, and even jellies and jams. What better way to try a $4.00 Chestnut Tea that you wouldn't normally buy because it's usually $9.00?

With Di$count stores, the more money you save while shopping, the more you can save for other things.

Swap/Trade Parties

This is one of my all-time favorites! Swap parties. I don't know who came up with the idea, but I have been doing them for years and have gotten some great pieces that way. I've recently begun doing "Swap Til You Drop" events, so be sure to look for one in your city!

The concept of swap parties is to get a group of friends together and each person has to bring items to swap. You must have an item to swap in order to receive a swap. Many swap parties have themes and some even allow you to bring small household items.

The swap parties I have are equipped with music, food, and wine. It's a great way to get something new and to socialize. The thing that makes swap parties stand above the rest is the fact you get "new" items for free.

You don't have to pay anything for these items. Just look in your closet or around your home and find something you don't want and would like to swap. If one person has a pair of shoes you want, and you have a jacket the other person wants, you swap them. You end up with items that are either new or "new" to you.

I have gotten items from Anthropologie, BCBG, Gucci, Louis Vuitton, and even Target! At my parties we draw numbers and go in order to pick the item we want, but if you want to swap with another person later, you are welcome to do so! This method works great for me, but you can find the method that will work best for you!

Swap parties help you save money because they allow you to get items without ever having to spend any! All you need are some items to swap and you can set up a swap party in your home!

Yard Sales and Flea Markets

This takes me back to days of my childhood. Sweet memories of getting up early on Saturday morning and going out with my mom to find the deal of the day! Yard sales and flea markets have been around forever.

The best thing about yard sales and flea markets is you never know what you will run into. Sometimes people don't even know what they are selling. There are countless stories of people buying artwork valued at thousands of dollars for pennies on the dollar or purchasing antiques for $5, $10, or $20!

Yard sales are usually done when a person is trying to get rid of "junk." Flea markets are where people take their "junk" to sell. One man's junk is another man's treasure! This is cool since the person having the sale thinks the items are junk and you can nickel and dime that seller. Besides, the object is to get rid of things. Nobody wants to pack that stuff up when it's over! This works in your favor in the negotiation department. Name your price and wait for a response.

There are all kinds of books that give tips on how to identify antiques and valuables. This might be worth looking into if you really want to get the full benefits of attending these sales.

You should look in your local newspaper for yard sales or flea markets in your area. Driving around neighborhoods can also help you identify sales in the area. There are also websites dedicated to identifying yard sales and flea markets, and some even list the items they are selling. You shouldn't have any problem finding them, as I have found flea markets even in Dubai!

The key to success is to get to the sales *early* in the morning as the best items get purchased first. For instance, if the sale starts at 7:00 am, you should try to get there at 6:45 am. The early bird definitely catches the worm in this case!

Yard sales and flea markets can help you save as long as you don't get the "Stuff Bug!" That's where you start going to them every weekend and start buying a whole bunch of stuff you don't want or need. If you do this, you will blow the concept of getting a deal because you are still spending a lot of money. You will have a whole bunch of stuff as opposed to a couple of items.

Estate Sales

Estate sales can be a great place to score deals. The idea behind them is that a person died and the heirs are trying to dispose of that person's things and also make some profit in the process. You can negotiate and get really good deals because the heirs don't want the items they are selling and nobody wants to pack all that stuff up at the end and take it to Goodwill.

The prices may be set at these sales or they may just ask you to make them an offer. Either way, I would wheel and deal and not just go with the price listed on the sticker. You don't know unless you ask, so ask and see if you can get a better deal.

The benefits of shopping estate sales is you can often find antique furniture, vintage clothing, and one-of-kind pieces for significantly less than purchasing them in a store. Some of the items may be out of your price range, but others may be right within budget.

I purchased a fur coat at an estate sale many years ago that I still receive compliments on even though I don't get to wear it much down south!

You can start looking for estate sales in your local newspaper. There will be many listed each week and you can narrow down your search by picking a particular area to visit. You can also look online. A few websites to visit are: www.estatesales.net, www.estatesaledirectory.com, and www.estatesale-finder.com.

The benefit of estate shopping is you can potentially find desirable luxury items without having to pay the luxury price. Di$count Diva's always get luxury for le$$.

Auctions

Auctions are a wonderful way to find everything from jewelry to home décor and furniture to cars to homes. Many of you have probably seen shows on T.V. like Auction Hunters, Auction Kings, Baggage Battles, and Storage Wars. Auctions have always been a big business, but now some of these shows let you know just how big it is.

Auctions can produce great deals because items are priced for a quick sale. There are all kinds of auctions from car auctions to storage unit auctions to home auctions. You should always arrive at auctions early as the phrase "the early bird catches the worm" is very true in this case.

Find out about storage unit auctions by checking with a local storage facility in your area. Be sure to inquire about payment for the unit. Is it required before you leave, do you have 24 hours to pay, and do they take checks? Also, find out how soon you have to have the items from the unit cleaned out. This is important because you may need to make arrangements to move large items prior to going to the auction.

When shopping for a car, bring a mechanic to inspect the vehicle before purchase. You don't want to purchase a car that looks like a shiny new penny on the outside, but is actually a lemon. You can find car auctions by looking on the internet or even contacting local dealerships. Many of them have auctions right on their grounds or send some of their cars to be auctioned monthly.

Since now is a great time to buy houses, don't forget to check the county courthouse for their monthly auctions. It's today (1st Tuesday of every month) throughout Georgia Counties. Remember, you may have to come prepared with cash or cashier's checks to purchase, depending on the county. Some cities like New York allow you to finance properties at auctions, but others do not. Check and find out when the local real estate auctions are in your area and what rules and restrictions apply.

When going to any auction it is important not to be timid or shy. You have to speak up if you want something. If you don't speak up, the sharks will definitely speak up. So be a little aggressive, or if you are not aggressive, then bring somebody with you who is!

Let auctions be a way you get things that you want for le$$, and when you get them, you can keep what you like and sell the rest!

Di$count Diva Tip # 19 -- Travel for Le$$

Traveling is one of the things I love to do most, and if you're like me you want to do it as often as possible. It makes sense to save money when traveling. Why would you pay high fees on flights, hotels, or rental cars when you can get them for significantly less by learning the tricks of travel and doing some research?

So, why would you pay a whole lot of money to travel to an exotic place if you can get there for 60% less? Or if you know you can only afford a $200 dollar plane ticket, then why aren't you trying to find a cheaper one? Come on people, saving money on travel only means more money to save or invest for something else.

OK now, Divas, so just how can you save on travel? Well, for one thing, you should look into discount travel websites, and there are a bunch out there from Best Fares to Booking Buddy to Hotwire, Orbitz, Priceline, and Travelocity, and the list goes on. You should also sign up for travel alerts. You can do this through many of the airlines as well as Vacations To Go or Travelzoo. This way you can put in your travel destination and get alerts sent as the price changes. These sites can save you a tremendous amount of cash, but be sure to check on whether or not you can make changes or refund your ticket if necessary.

You can also maximize money by signing up for frequent flyer programs. Pretty much all airlines offer frequent flyer miles, so make sure to sign up for their programs and even look into credit cards and banking programs that offer travel incentives. Make sure you check with the programs for blackout days so you are aware of when you can and cannot travel.

Another way to save on travel is by taking advantage of "last minute" sales on flights, hotels, and car rentals. These prices usually entail you traveling in the very near future, possibly the upcoming weekend, so you need a flexible schedule to take advantage of them, but if you are spontaneous and have the money, you could be in Miami this weekend. If you can't fly "last minute," one of the oldest tricks of the trade is to purchase airline tickets to depart on Tuesdays or Thursdays. These are the best days to buy tickets.

Being flexible on the days you can travel by leaving a day earlier or staying a day later can also make all the difference in the world with pricing, and staying somewhere seven days may actually cost less than staying four days. With all the recent nickel and diming by the airlines, I would also suggest you bring a carry-on so you don't have to pay the baggage fee. Also, look into airlines that don't charge such fees, like Southwest.

If you're 18-22 years old, there are also great programs geared towards college students, e.g., Airtran U, where you can fly for super cheap, or consider traveling using Mega Bus. You can travel for as little as $3 per leg of your trip, and Mega Bus also offers free Wi-Fi and an area at your seat to charge cell phones or computers.

Remember, the money you save from the tips above should be saved or invested. It's not a true Di$count if you don't keep the difference!

6 CHAPTER
ELIMINATING DEBT

Di$count Diva Tip #20 -- Get Out of "Bad Debt"

I know many of us have heard this before. The way to building wealth is to get out of debt, but there is a difference between "Good Debt" and "Bad Debt." Bad debt is anything that takes money out of your pocket, e.g., your residential property, credit cards, or automobiles. Good debt is debt that puts or has the potential to put money into your pocket, e.g., student loans, rental properties, or business loans.

Let's examine this more closely. Most of us have been told, "Your home is your biggest investment," but is it really an investment? In light of the recent mortgage crisis we are being enlightened to the truth. We have seen home prices drop tremendously over the last six years, and all of the astronomical gains that were made during the housing boom are now a bust. Many homeowners are now underwater, owing more on their homes than they are worth and many don't see a way out. Some homeowners have gone as far as settling for short sales, deed in lieu, or even allowing their properties to foreclose just to get out of the homes.

You have to ask yourself, would people be worried about their homes if they were actually good debt? I don't think so. People are concerned because they've been told the lie that their personal home is an asset and now they've seen all the decline in their equity; however, if this were an investment property, or good debt, you wouldn't care, because you would have someone else in the home paying the mortgage and creating an additional income stream. The advantage of an investment property is that at some point you will pay it off and continue to earn income on it or sell it for a profit down the line, so drops in prices on investment properties need not be devastating.

What about cars? We all pretty much know once you drive a car off the lot it immediately starts to lose value. That's why I recommend buying used cars, especially if you like high-end or luxury cars. Cars lose most of their value the first three years, so why pay all that money for the new car smell? They sell spray for that! A car like a home is something you will continually maintain, so it's definitely not good debt. So what is the solution? Pay off that car as soon as possible, finance for no more than three years, and get the lowest rates by maintaining a high credit score.

So just what is a credit score? It's the score that you are given based on how you have paid past credit obligations, the length of time you have had credit accounts, the assets you own, and numerous other variables. It's kind of like a report card for your credit where 740 and up is an A and anything under 620 would be a D or an F. It's important to maintain a high score because it will impact the interest you are charged on everything from homes, to cars, to credit cards, and may even cause you to pay deposits on things like cell phones and utilities. The higher your score, the less you will pay for the things.

The worst kind of credit is credit card debt. You don't have *anything* to show for that as far as being good debt is concerned. Buying on credit most of the time means you can't afford it and credit card companies know this, but they benefit from allowing you to "borrow" money to fulfill your need for instant gratification. This does come at a cost, sometimes even up to 29% interest so that store card you open up to save 15% doesn't save you a penny, unless you pay it off in full at the end of the month.

Credit card debt puts no money into your pocket and will always be considered bad debt *unless* you are using it for the benefit of an asset, like paying for books for college. Even then I would prefer you get a student loan at a much lower interest rate. Some people use credit cards to buy real estate, but I wouldn't advise this unless you really know what you are doing!

Good debt like student loans can put money into your pocket because you are taking out the loans to get a degree or certification that will help you advance yourself and make more money. Student loans can become bad debt when you are taking out more money than you know you can reasonably pay back based on the expected salary for your future job. This is where being R.E.A.L. comes in. Don't take out $30,000 a year to go to a private institution to get a four-year degree in an area where you will only make $50,000 a year. Why should you take out $120,000 for that degree when you can go to a less pricey school and take out half or only a quarter of that amount? Remember to *always* pay your student loans. I had to learn this lesson the hard way. Not repaying student loans is one of the easiest ways to wreck your credit. Think of it this way. If you gave someone a loan, you would want it back, right? Well, maybe you could let one loan go, but what if you gave millions of people loans? Could you afford to let millions of loans go unpaid? Neither can the government or private lenders!

Business loans can be good debt because you are taking them out to expand and grow your venture. Be sure you adequately plan for periods of time when you might not be making much money, and be ready to plug a large chunk of your profits back into the business or to the repayment of your loan in the first few years.

Business credit is different from other kinds; however, if you default on a business loan it can have an impact on your personal credit score.

As you are paying off bad debt it can be important to find additional opportunities to create good debt, especially if that is part of your wealth building plan, so get out and stay out of bad debt!

Di$count Diva Tip #21-- Pay off Revolving and Installment Debt

Revolving debt is any debt where the payment amount can "revolve" or change from month to month. Revolving debts are credit cards because your minimum payment may be $20 or $200. This amount will depend on the amount of the balance and will decrease as you pay it down and increase as you add new purchases.

Credit cards are designed to keep you in debt for long periods of time if you only make the minimum payment. The object should be to pay off these cards as soon as possible. You can do this by calling your credit card company and finding out the **APR** on each card. APR is the **annual percentage rate,** and it takes into account the interest rate *plus* any additional fees like annual fees, monthly fees, and balance transfer fees. Once you have figured out your APR on all cards, target the card with the highest APR and pay an extra $50-$100 on top of your minimum payment, but only pay the minimum payments on the other accounts. Once that first card is paid off, take the extra money you were paying on it and apply it to the second card. Once the second card is paid off, apply the money from the first and second cards to the third card and so on until all cards are paid off.

You may also want to threaten your card company to close your account or transfer your balance to another card. Now you are not really going to close this account, but if you tell them you are or that you have received an offer from another company offering 0% interest for 12 months, they will probably be willing to negotiate. If you have been a long-time customer and have paid on time, they will probably also be willing to *reward* you by lowering your interest rate. This will definitely help you pay off your cards quicker.

Installment debt like car loans, student loans, and personal loans are debts that offer a set amount for the monthly payment, and this remains the same from month to month. For example, if you have a car loan, your payment may be $440/month and it is that same amount each month. You may have a student loan and that amount will be the same each month.

You can pay off your car faster by adding extra money to your car payment each month. Try to pay an extra $50-$100 each month, but be sure to let the car company know the extra amount is for principal reduction and not for interest. Also, it can sometimes be a benefit to refinance your car loan if you can get a lower interest rate and keep the current terms of your loan. It is not a benefit if you have a three-year loan and you are going to refinance to a five-year loan.

Student loans can be paid off quicker by consolidating them into one low interest loan. There are many companies and websites that do this. Research your best options, because once you consolidate, you may not be able to reconsolidate.

You can also sign up for automatic drafts. Some loan companies reduce your interest rate by signing up for automatic drafts by a half percent, and every bit helps! If you are working in a helping profession like teaching, counseling, or medicine, you may want to check out programs that will reduce or eliminate some of your student loans if you work in certain areas that need your expertise.

After you pay off all credit cards and installment loans, take the amount you were paying towards these debts and place it in an emergency fund or investment vehicle. If you do this, when you have another emergency, you won't have to place it on a credit card and get back into debt. Also, you may be able to buy your next vehicle for cash, or at least have a sizeable down payment.

Di$count Diva Tip #22 -- Take Advantage of Credit Card Points

There are many incentives credit card companies are now offering to customers to keep their business. Some offer rewards that can be exchanged for things like flights, hotels, gas, and even cash back.

Since credit is often necessary to operate in this world, why not get a card that offers rewards and incentives. You can also check with your bank, as many banks now offer points and incentives as well.

Some of the top credit cards that offer the best incentives include:

Citi Dividend Platinum Select Visa

- $100 cash back after $500 in purchases within the first three months of account opening.
- Earn 5% cash back from Citi on eligible purchases at Zappos.com, fitness clubs and drugstores from 1/1/13 through 3/31/13 when you enroll.
- 0% Intro APR on Balance Transfers and Purchases for 12 months. After that, the APR will be 12.99%-22.99% variable based on your creditworthiness*
- Enroll at no additional cost each quarter for new categories that earn additional cash back
- Full 1% cash back on all other purchases and eligible cash advances.
- No annual fee*

This card actually won an Editor's Choice Award, so in order to get this card you need to have excellent credit. Now what do I mean by excellent? Anyone under a 700 need not apply.

Chase Freedom Visa

- Earn $100 bonus cash back after you make $500 in purchases in your first three months.

- 0% Intro APR for 15 months on purchases and balance transfers.

- 5% cash back on up to $1,500 spent between Jan 1 and Mar 31, 2013 at gas stations, drugstores, and Starbucks® stores.

- New 5% categories every three months like gas stations, restaurants, and Amazon.com. It's free and easy to activate your bonus each quarter!

- Unlimited 1% cash back on all other purchases.

- No annual fee and rewards never expire.

Capital One Venture One Rewards Card

(You've probably seen the ads by now with the catch phrase, "What's in your wallet?")

- Earn double miles with every purchase toward free flights on any airline.

- "Most Rewarding Card if you crave free airline flights" - Money® Magazine, 5/11/2011

- Earn 10,000 bonus miles when you spend $1,000 on purchases within the first three months, equal to $100 in travel.

- Redeem your miles for any travel expense.

- No limit on the miles you can earn and miles don't expire.

- Fly on any airline, any time with no blackout dates.

- No foreign transaction fees.
- $0 intro annual fee for the first year, $59 after that.

American Express Gold Card

(For those of you who love the idea of never paying any interest while using a charge card. You must have excellent credit to get this, but remember, this is not a credit card, it is a charge card. You will not be charged *any* interest; however, the balance will be due in full each month. This card is great for forcing discipline by letting you know not to put anything on there you can't pay off in 30 days.)

- Earn Everyday: earn 1X point for every dollar you spend on purchases with unlimited earning potential and earn 10X points with select retailers at membershiprewards.com/earn.Travel Rewards: use Pay with Points to book flights, cruises, hotels, and vacation packages with no seat restrictions or blackout dates on americanexpress.com/travel.Access to Exclusive Protections: enjoy Baggage Insurance Plan*when you travel, and shop with confidence with Extended Warranty*, Purchase Protection*, and Return Protection. *Underwritten by Amex Assurance Company.Redeem with Flexibility: use points for gift cards for dining, entertainment, and to shop for over 300 of some of your favorite brands.$0 introductory annual fee for the first year, then $125.Terms and restrictions Apply.

There are many more cards that offer incentives, rewards, and benefits. You can do a search or go to www.CreditCards.com or www.bankrate.com to find the right card for you. You can compare APR, fees, conditions, restrictions, and incentives all on one site. If you currently have a card that offers sky miles that you are not taking advantage of, you can sell those miles for cash at: www.earnrewardscash.com.

Be sure to make it a point to save any money you get back from your cards to increase your emergency fund, add to your IRA, or place in an interest-bearing account. And if you have a balance on your card, use the money to pay off your balance.

The key is to not get entangled in buying more than you really need just to earn incentives, or putting everything on your credit card to earn rewards and then not paying it off and racking up interest charges. So, making this work for you requires discipline.

Take advantage of credit. Don't let it take advantage of you.

Lynesha McElveen

7 CHAPTER
ACCUMULATING ASSETS

Di$count Diva Tip #23 -- Try Non-Traditional Investments

There are many options out there for investing for our futures.
Most times, people go with the obvious, such as investing in their
company **401K** or starting an **IRA (Individual Retirement
Account)**, buying mutual funds/stock, and purchasing real estate.

While I am a big fan of real estate, why not learn about some non-
traditional ways to invest, e.g. using **OPM (Other People's
Money), and investing in notes, short sales, tax lien certificates,
gold,** and/or **commodities.** There are even investment groups
where you can directly lend money to individuals and earn up to
24% interest.

In light of the recent changes in mortgage lending, many investors
have had to learn creative ways to finance their purchases. As a
former loan officer, I personally witnessed the lending standards
change from, "Anyone with a pulse can get a loan, i.e., NINA-No
Income No Assets," to "You have to give a pint of blood, your
first-born, and your right arm to get a loan, i.e., people with over
720 scores not qualifying, no longer being able to add back write-
offs to your income, and having to supply the bank statements of a

person offering gift funds to prove that the giver can afford to provide the money!"

I have also watched investors get denied who could easily go into the bank and get loans and who had done so for decades. Because of this, it was necessary for them to find innovative ways to finance their investments. Now, I am sharing some of these secrets with you.

OPM, which was first mentioned, is using Other People's Money. I first heard about it from real estate investor Carlton Sheets. The idea is to get the money for purchasing real estate from others. You can do this by asking people you know who have lazy money sitting around. For example, right now the interest paid on CDs and savings accounts are extremely low. There are plenty of people who would rather make 10% or 12% by investing their money with you than the 1% or less it is making at the bank.

There are people who have come into large lump sums and are afraid to risk it in the stock market or who have retired and are looking for a monthly cash flow amount. These may be some prime investors you can use to purchase real estate.

You might also want to try investing in **notes**. A note is a legally binding document between a seller and a buyer where the buyer promises to repay borrowed money according to the terms that have been established. Buying a note is buying debt. Notes are nothing new as banks commonly buy notes as an ordinary and traditional business practice.

Here are some steps to follow when buying a note. First, do a search on owners of notes; second, call the owner and let them know you are interested in buying the note; third, obtain the original documents executed when the note was created; fourth, find out the current value of the home to ensure that the home value will cover the note; and fifth, run a credit check on the seller to find out if there are any pending foreclosures.

There are other ways you can buy notes, including **peer-to-peer investing** or **crowd funding.** This has become extremely popular in the last few years. People use this method that don't want to go to traditional banks or may not be able to do so. By setting up a profile with a company that provides this service, they enable average, everyday people to fund their loans.

People who desire to borrow money through this medium may need it to reconsolidate debt, do home additions, start a business, or even fund a wedding. You as an investor decide where you are willing to put your money and which notes you want to buy.

The investors are paid back in small increments, and the time it takes to be fully repaid depends on the terms of the note. Investors can make upwards of 20% using these resources. As with traditional investments, the higher the risk, the potentially higher the return, and vice versa. Some companies to look at for buying notes include Lending Club and Kickstarter, the world's largest funding platform for creative projects.

Remember, as with any investment, there is risk involved. I have an account with Lending Club and I have 19 notes. All of them were paying extremely well and I had interest ranging from 7% to 24%, but one of the notes recently defaulted and was charged off. That is money I will never get. The good thing is that with Lending Club you can invest as little as $25, so you don't need a lot of money to get started, and the potential loss on a $25 note is much less severe than on thousand dollar investments elsewhere.

Tax lien certificates and **tax sales** are great ways to come up with a piece of property or to achieve a high return on your investment in a relatively short period of time. In buying tax liens, you are paying the property taxes of the owner and are given a guaranteed interest rate. The idea is that the homeowner has a set period of time to repay the taxes or you own the property. Typically, this period is one year. If the owner repays the taxes, then you will get a hefty interest rate on your money, possibly over 20%; if the owner doesn't repay the taxes in a year, you own the property. This can be tricky because sometimes people will bid the taxes up. For example, if there is a $300,000 home that owes $27,000 in taxes, a person may want to buy the taxes for $60,000. It is possible that you may not be able to buy the taxes in this case unless you have significant amounts of cash to invest. However, if you do, then if the owner redeems the home, you will make possibly $12,000-$15,000 on your money in a year. That's a good deal!

You also want to be sure you know what you are getting into. Often people invest in tax liens just for the interest, thinking they will get their money back when the owner defaults. From then on that property is your responsibility to pay the taxes on and to maintain. Now, you could obviously rent it out, if it is in rentable condition, but you may have to put some money into the home to get it up to par. This is something to consider when buying liens.

Di$count Diva Tip #24 -- Get Rich Investing 20%

In order to get rich you must consistently invest in a vehicle that is producing a decent return (minimum 8%), but then you may ask, "How much should I invest?" Experts say in order to retire well you should invest a minimum of 10%; however to retire rich you must invest 15-20% of your take-home pay. You are probably thinking, "Where am I gonna get 20% to invest?" Start by decreasing things like daily eat-out lunches, frivolous shopping, buying things you don't need or want, and cutting costs on things like cell and home phone bills. If you aren't able to save 10%, start at 1% and work your way up. Something is better than nothing!

Investing in **gold** has been a big trend lately. If you live in my area, you have seen the "We Buy Gold" stores popping up everywhere. This is because gold is at an "all time high" according to analysts. This is a great time to sell gold for profit, but is it a good time to buy gold? It depends on whom you ask. Some say that gold will continue to rise, so it is good to buy it and sell later; others say the price is too high, so wait until it starts to decline to buy. Whatever the case, buying precious metals can be an additional way to accumulate assets.

Other things to look at are **commodities.** Commodities are things like wood, oil, cattle, and even coffee and orange juice. Wikipedia defines commodities as a marketable item used to satisfy a need or want and is comprised of goods and services. The thing about buying commodities is there are things that people most always will need, so there will probably always be a market for them. Commodities can be a great way to diversify a traditional portfolio of stocks and can be traded online through various trading companies.

A popular way to buy commodities is through a **futures contract**. This is an agreement in which the investor commits to buy a specific amount at a specific price in the future. Doing this type of deal is known as speculation, because you are speculating on what the price will be in the future, whether higher or lower. There are pros and cons to investing in commodities and using futures contracts. You can easily make big profits if you are on the right side of the trade, but the futures market can be very volatile and risky for inexperienced investors. As always, do your homework, and if you are interested in investing this way, learn as much as you can before getting involved.

There are many ways to invest for your future. Some ways may be more comfortable to you than others, so the key is to find the best fit for you and be willing to look at some non-traditional means of making money!

Di$count Diva Tip #25 -- Invest in Real Estate

This can include buying single family or multifamily homes with your money or with the help of banks and investors. It can also include buying commercial properties like office space, apartments, or buildings. Of course, you have land contracts you can purchase, which come in handy if you know the plans for a particular area. For example, many people got rich in Atlanta by buying up homes and land around the airport. The Hartsfield-Jackson Airport is the busiest airport in the world, so when the airport needed space to expand, many of those surrounding homes and lands had to be purchased. This was an example of profiting by being in "the know."

Investing in real estate can range from **short sales** to **wholesaling,** and can include **HUD properties** and **foreclosure properties**. It can involve using **quit claim deeds** or just identifying homes that are undervalued and buying them well below cost. You may also choose to flip them, which is to buy a property and fix it quickly for immediate resale, or to buy and hold it for consistent monthly income. Whatever you choose, it's up to you what will work best for you. Let's explore a couple of the options.

Buying single family homes is typically where people start. They identify a home they like, go to a bank for a loan, and purchase the home. Many tend to buy the home for retail price, but in order to profit, it's important to buy it for well under value, $0.40 on the $1.00 if possible. The idea is to buy the property low and sell high because property always goes up in value, right? In light of our recent mortgage experience we've seen properties actually lose value, and people are under water right now. If you are buying for cash flow, meaning you are buying to get a monthly rental income, then it won't matter. For example, if you buy a home at $100,000 and the value drops to $60,000, you probably don't want to sell it, but you can rent it. If you were getting $1,000/month rent when the value was $100,000, you can still get $1,000 when the value is $60,000.

Another avenue is buying multifamily properties. This includes duplexes, triplexes, quads, and small and large apartment buildings. This can be cool because you have more units to get rent from and you don't need all of the units to be filled for cash flow. For example, if you have an eight unit apartment building, and only six apartments are filled at $800/month, and your mortgage is $3,500, your situation is still positive because you're making $4,800, even though two units are vacant. You can also use the triplex method to pay your own mortgage by living in one side and renting out the other. If done right, this will cover your entire mortgage on the property. Using this concept, many homeowners are electing to redo their basements as apartments.

What about buying commercial properties? Commercial properties can be a tremendous benefit. First of all, people usually sign multiyear leases. Also, many commercial properties make the tenants responsible for fixing maintenance problems. I have a friend looking for space in Atlanta for a daycare who was told she would have to fix HVAC if she leased the property; and another friend in Florida who was told she would have to fix the plumbing for a hair salon. This is great for the owners of those properties. So if you own commercial real estate, you don't have as much to worry about in maintenance fees as you do with residential property. Plus, tenants are less likely to tear up office and commercial space.

You can purchase properties many ways, and one of those ways is a **short sale.** A short sale occurs when a property owner owes more on the home than it is worth. The owner may not be able to sell the home in traditional ways due to being in default or to property values going down. For instance, if someone bought a home at $130,000 but because of foreclosures in the area the values are now between $89,000 and $110,000, then you as an investor petition the bank to let you buy the home for the new value. Does this really happen? It does, but sometimes not in a quick manner. My own experience was I lost a home in Charlotte, NC after I had a buyer who wanted to purchase by means of a short sale, but the bank wouldn't get back to us. The numbers I mention are real. The buyer was willing to pay $110,000, but I owed $127,000 and the bank wouldn't approve it.

Don't get me wrong. Short sales can be an awesome way to get a home for a lot less than you normally would have to pay, but it can be a lengthy process. Some banks are taking months and even up to a year to approve a short sale, so when using this investment approach, you must have time on your side.

Wholesaling allows you to buy a property with little cash or credit. A wholesaler will buy a property, typically distressed, and sell it to another investor. The advantage is that the price overcomes any objections about the condition of the property. For example, if you find a property for $23,000 that was worth over $100,000, it doesn't matter that it needs a new roof. An investor will put the new roof on it for $15,000, pay you a few thousand to wholesale it to him, and buy the property. Sounds too good to be true, huh? It's not. It's happening in my area and probably in yours too every day!

So what about **HUD** or **REO** properties? A HUD home is a property acquired by the Department of Housing and Urban Development as a result of a foreclosure on an FHA-insured mortgage. HUD homes may allow you to finance money for repairs into the loan and will require that the home is up to standard before selling it to you. An REO or Real Estate Owned property is a property that is bank owned. REOs are sold "as is" with the buyer taking on all the responsibilities of the property.

In buying **foreclosures,** you want to identify a realtor or broker who works directly with banks that own foreclosed properties. Get a pre-approval from a lender if you are financing traditionally. A mistake is thinking that just because the bank is selling you the home they will finance it. If you are using non-traditional means, identify investment money. Find a contractor to do maintenance on the home.

Quit claim deeds allow you to buy a property from someone who may be in trouble with their mortgage, may need to move all of a sudden, or may have a home that is just sitting vacant. The benefit is that the person remains on the loan, if there is one, and they deed the property over to you. You then own the property without having to do anything to finance or get credit for the home. You will owe only what is left on the loan, or if it is owned free and clear you own it outright. This approach typically works well with people who are trying to get out of a home quickly or because they can't make the repairs.

Remember, most likely you will have to put some money into these homes, and many of these strategies allow you to buy properties at a discount. You only benefit from real estate if you purchase it for less than it is worth and a true Di$count Diva only purchases things for less than they are worth!

Di$count Diva Tip #26 -- Invest in a Business: Consider Network Marketing

Everyone thinks that owning a business is so difficult and too expensive. Most of us think of traditional brick and mortar businesses, like owning a franchise of a restaurant, or opening a book store or car wash. You are right, owning a business can be hard, but it doesn't necessarily have to be expensive.

There are many ways you can own a business with small to minimal investment. This can include **multilevel** or **network marketing.** Network marketing often gets a bad reputation as people refer to them as "pyramid schemes," citing that the people who make money are at the top and everybody on the bottom doesn't make that much. But in actuality aren't all businesses pyramids? Doesn't the CEO of Coca-Cola make a lot more money than the plant worker and the driver? What about the president of Bank of America or Porsche? Don't they make more money than the teller and the car salesman? The truth is, business is a pyramid. The manager of a McDonald's makes more than the fry girl, and the district manager makes more than the manager, and the person who owns a few McDonald's franchises makes more than them all. This is how business works, so now that you've got that out of your mind don't be afraid to take a look at a network marketing company.

Like all businesses, they involve start-up costs, so be sure to factor that in to your projected expenses. You need to think of things like materials, space, and employee salaries, not to mention licenses, corporate fees, bank fees, and payroll expenses.

The reason network marketing companies are great is that they have few start-up costs. Many you can start with as little as $499 and some companies even run specials where you can start for as low as $99. The thing I love about these companies is many are committed to making sure you earn back your initial investment in the company within the first 30 days. They know if you don't make any money, you will quit and in order for them to make money, they have to help you make money. Teamwork makes the dream work!

Other benefits are the personal development that takes place during the process of learning how to manage a business. You overcome the fear of rejection, learn to sell, learn how to overcome objections, and become a "better you" in the process. Network marketing companies often encourage reading books and articles by profound teachers like John Maxwell, Zig Ziglar, and Jim Rohn, all great business developers in their own right.

Network marketing allows you to grow yourself while growing your business in the process, and you can do all of this without investing a whole lot of money. That way, if the venture doesn't work out, you won't have lost a significant amount of money.

In any business it's important to look for things like residual income. Residual income for a business owner is like syndication for an actor or royalties for a singer. You do something one time, but you get paid for it over and over again. An example of this can be if you have a company that sells cable services or health care services that pays a residual. You get a small percentage of the amount paid monthly by every client that signs up with you. You might have signed them up for cable one time, but every time they pay their bill you make money.

Also, if you invest in a network marketing company, look into whether or not the business has stock options or other incentives. Can the business be willed to a family member? Do they offer car vouchers? These are important items to think about when deciding how the business can best benefit you and help you reach your financial goals. In addition to the business providing increased income, you also get tremendous tax deductions, hence putting more money in your pocket. Business ownership is a good way to take your income to the next level while providing you with a sense of personal satisfaction and helping you grow.

8 CHAPTER
PROTECTING ASSETS

Di$count Diva Tip #27 -- Get a Will

So you don't think you have a lot to leave behind, don't have children, or aren't a millionaire? That doesn't mean you don't have things other people see as valuable or are willing to fight and fall out over. A **will** puts things in writing, makes your intentions clear, and leaves less confusion during an already stressful time. It puts everything into perspective so people don't have to worry about trivial and material things while dealing with the death of a loved one. Besides, why do you want your family arguing over whom your china goes to, or your prized Chanel bag, or your car? You can nip all of this in the bud by making a will.

We've probably all heard the phrase, "Where there's a will, there's a way," but I say, "Where there's not a will, the State will have its way." In other words, if you don't decide where you want your assets to go, the state will decide, with many of your assets going to it! It's called Intestate.

So why don't people make wills? Wills can often be expensive by requiring an attorney. But there are many less expensive ways to accomplish this goal. You can use companies like Legalzoom or if you have a prepaid legal service, they will often put a will together for you free of charge as part of your package. So, you may be paying $20 a month for the service and get a free will done every three years or so.

Also, there are will kits you can buy at retailers like Office Depot and Staples that can walk you through formulation of a basic will. These allow you to complete the will yourself; however, I would still recommend you having an attorney review it.

You should also consider a **living will**. A living will has nothing to do with assets, but everything to do with allowing people to make medical decisions for you. Living wills allow you to be in control of your medical treatment even when you are not able to verbalize what you want. For example, if you want a **DNR (Do Not Resuscitate)** you can put this in your living will. Most times, your family members will be too emotionally charged to make that decision and you don't want them to have to! To make sure your orders are followed you need a **durable power of attorney for health care** and **an advanced directive.** This way your wishes will most definitely be followed because of the legally binding steps you've taken.

Di$count Diva Tip #28 -- Establish a Trust

There are a number of legal entities you can set up to protect yourself and your assets. They can range from **annuities** to **trusts.** While a will tells people where you want your assets to go upon your death, a **living revocable trust** allows someone to make financial decisions while you are alive in the event you are incapacitated. For example, what happens if you get sick to the point where you are unable to speak and your family needs to use your money to get nursing home care or to have an in-home health aide come in? If you don't have a living revocable trust established, they won't be able to touch your money. This could truly affect the care you receive.

If you are afraid that establishing a trust will allow someone else access to your money, you can stipulate that you are the trustee and that another person you have designated becomes successor trustee if you become incapacitated. Establishing a living revocable trust also makes it easier to get money to your heirs without going through probate court, which will most assuredly eat up a large portion of your money.

You will also want to choose a **guardian** for your children. If you don't pick a guardian, you are leaving it up to the state to choose. It may choose the person you want, but it may not. That's the risk you take if you don't select a legal guardian.

If you have established funds for your child for college, such as by using a **529 College Savings Plan,** you can name the child as the first beneficiary and the **529 Plan Trust** as the successor beneficiary. This way you will ensure any money left for your children for college will get to them for just that purpose. The 529 is a tax advantaged investment vehicle designed to encourage savings for future higher education.

It's always important to consider the ones we love. A Di$count Diva always makes sure that even in her absence things will run smoothly. Di$count Divas handle business both while alive on earth and while here in spirit. So, handle your business and get a will and trust!

Di$count Diva Tip #29 -- Insurance...The First Line of Defense

The types of **insurance** you can set up to protect your assets in the event of death, unemployment, or disability can be staggering. They can range from **mortgage protection insurance to disability insurance**. There is also **life insurance,** which will provide a check to your heirs to cover living expenses and help them continue to fund their current lifestyle in the event of your demise. The best advice is to speak with a legal and/or financial professional about the best way to protect and maintain your assets during life's ups and downs.

Mortgage Protection Insurance

While **private mortgage insurance (PMI)** protects the *lender* in the event you default or foreclose as a borrower, mortgage protection insurance protects *you* in the event you can't pay your mortgage. Mortgage protection is designed to pay your mortgage for you in the event of things like unemployment, disability, or even death. This protects *you* so if you are unable to pay your mortgage because you are sick or out of work, you won't lose your home; and it protects your heirs because if you die and there is a balance left on your home, they won't lose their place to live. If you don't want mortgage insurance, be sure to have enough money as part of your life insurance package to cover the payoff of your mortgage.

Short Term Disability Insurance

While women now make up 49.35% of the workforce, they also make up 69.3% of the breadwinners, according to The Center for American Progress. In 2005, 78% of people working were eligible for leave under the Family Medical Leave Act (FMLA) during that year. Women are also three times more likely to suffer a disability than men. That being said, short term disability insurance is something that is very important, especially for women. It is great to be able to take the time off work without fear of losing your job, but isn't it even better if you can get paid in the process?

Short term disability insurance may allow you to take extra time off work after having a complicated pregnancy or to get extra care after surgery. It will cover between 50%-100% of your living expenses while you are out of work.

I have many friends who have benefited from companies like Aflac and who swear by them. Some have gotten thousands of dollars after being out of work from surgeries, and others have gotten hundreds of dollars just in wellness checks for getting regular check-ups.

While long term disability payments from Social Security will kick in after you are disabled for six months, short term disability insurance will take care of those first few months. It is something you cannot go without and no self-respecting Di$count Diva would try to do so.

Long Term Disability Insurance

While many may argue that you don't have a need for long term disability insurance, I see it differently. Some think, "Well, if I get disabled I can just apply for Social Security Disability" and you can, but how many of us would be able to live off the meager amount of money we would receive from government disability? I know I wouldn't.

Long term disability insurance like any insurance is a way to put you back even. It's a way to ensure if you were disabled for a long period of time, you wouldn't lose your assets, and you would be able to eat and pay your bills. It's not to make sure you go on vacations, or can get the latest designer handbag, Divas, so you might have to make some adjustments to your spending.

You can get long term disability insurance several different ways. You can purchase the kind that only kicks in after you have been disabled for a year, 18 months, and so forth. I know you may be thinking, "How am I gonna make it a year without income?" If you have put your emergency fund in place, then being disabled would be considered an "emergency" and this would be the time you could live off that, if you didn't have short term disability insurance.

If you are a member of a company or a trade organization, try to see if you can apply for benefits through them. It's much less expensive, and I know we are all about discounts! If you do apply through your job, make sure it's a benefit you can transfer and take with you in the event you leave the job or the company. Once you get long term disability insurance, make sure to pay the premiums. This is something that could be the difference between surviving life's challenges or going into financial ruin. Get long term disability insurance!

Life Insurance
Maybe you haven't been there. Someone dies, and there is no money available to bury the deceased. People are pooling their money together, putting expenses on charge cards, and even passing around money jars. This doesn't have to be, especially when you can often get term life insurance for pennies on the dollar.

For example, a 29-year-old woman can get a $700,000, 35-year term life insurance policy for as little as $50/month. In order to get this great rate, you must qualify based on your health, but even a 56-year-old smoker with high blood pressure can get a 20-year term policy of $30,000 for about $34/month. You may able to find rates even lower.

The idea of life insurance is to protect your assets and your family while you are building wealth. I am a fan of term insurance because you can get much larger amounts for a lot less than with a whole life plan, and you can invest the difference. For instance, if you want to purchase a million dollar policy and you are a 30-year-old healthy woman, you may be able to get that with a 35-year term policy for $79; however, if you try to purchase a million dollar whole life policy you will be paying $1,000 or more a month.

Don't think you need a million dollars in insurance? Maybe you don't, but you should get at least 10-20 times your annual salary in insurance. So if you make $50,000 a year, you should purchase between $500,000 and $1,000,000 in life insurance.

It's not a question of *if* you are going to die but *when* and *what the consequences will be for your loved ones.* Life insurance allows you to take care of your family after you are gone. What better gift can you give to your family than financial security, knowing they don't have to move out of the home they grew up in, or won't be able to go to college because Mom's gone? Life insurance allows you to help financially from the grave, plus it's the number one way wealth is transferred in the United States.

No one who cherishes their family would leave them holding the bag, so why would you leave yours like that? And with the price of term insurance so low, there is no reason why a Di$count Diva wouldn't protect her family!

Di$count Diva Tip #30 -- Giving: The Best Insurance on the Market

I know many people don't think they have enough money to donate to someone else. Many think they are struggling and that giving to others will put them in a financially binding situation. Don't even get me started on **tithing.** A tithe or "the tenth" is 10% of something. In financial terms, it's a dime off a dollar. Some of you may be thinking that's nothing, but if you got a bonus at work of $10,000, would you be willing to tithe $1,000? Others of you may be thinking, "I'll do it when I make more money." The truth of the matter is, if you don't do it off the little, you won't do it off the much. If it's hard to tithe when you make $2,500 a month by giving $250, what do you think it will feel like when you make $5,000 a month and that tithe is now $500?

Some just don't see the benefit in giving away 10% of their hard-earned money, but there are many benefits to tithing and giving back. Tithing and giving put you in a position to receive. There is a proverb that says, *"There is one that scatters, and yet increases; and there is one that withholds more than is right, but it leads to poverty."* In other words, if you wonder why the rich keep getting richer it is because many of them are huge givers/contributors to others. If you try to clench your money too tightly, it will just slip through your fingers, whereas if you are willing to give it away to others, you may see how it comes back to you over and beyond what you gave away.

I'm not a drill sergeant when it comes to whom you tithe to. Some think you should only tithe to a religious group or assembly. I believe you should be led by the Spirit on how and whom you give to. I mean, if your mother is about to get put out of her home, would you tithe or would you help your mother? Scripture also says, *"Give to anyone who asks and do not turn them away,"* Matthew 5:42. Also *"Do not withhold good from those who deserve it when it is in your power to act. Do not tell your neighbor come back tomorrow and I'll give it to you then,"* Proverbs 3:27-28.

From personal experience, I know the benefits of tithing and giving. There have been times I tithed and didn't know how I was going to eat, and someone came up to me after I had made a gift and offered to take me out to dinner. Tithing is what got me a full scholarship to graduate school, where I received over $4,000 a month from grants and scholarships with only $550 in expenses.

Giving is what continues to promote me in my life. It's never a question for me. If I see a homeless person with a sign who is asking for money and I feel led, I give it. I don't question what they will do with the money. That is not my concern or my issue. My issue is to give to everyone who asks and know that it will be multiplied to me. I don't give to get. I give because I would want someone to give to me if I was in need, and when I have been in need, people have given to me.

I don't lend money to people. When I say "people," I mean friends and family. People have asked me for loans in the past, and I have given them, but I never expect to be repaid. If the person repays me, great! If the person doesn't, that's fine too. Either way I will be blessed for my gift, and the feeling I get from helping others is priceless.

If you still are not keen on letting go of money, try giving away your talents and skills or donating time to a worthy cause. Spend a couple of hours a week volunteering at a shelter, or helping with battered women, or mentoring a child. Outside of helping someone else, the joy you feel from doing something good far outweighs any money you could receive.

Tithe your talents and skills by finding organizations that need your skill set and work with them for free. For example, if you know how to sew, find an organization that does handmade quilts for abused or hospitalized children. If you are a hairstylist or beauty expert, volunteer to do hair, makeup, nails, or styling for women seeking employment. You may be able to find some of these women by contacting the Department of Labor in your area. Go here this site http://www.dol.gov/ to find your local headquarters.

Make sure when you are giving of your tithe, you do it without expecting anything in return. The way the system works, you will get the best **ROI (Return on Investment)** than with anything else you could have ever invested in.

Remember when volunteering to discount yourself and remain humble. You never want to appear better than those you are serving. A Di$count Diva always knows how to give to others and contribute to the lives of those in need in a manner that is gracious and considerate.

9 CHAPTER
GET R.E.A.L. ™

So now that we've gone through the 30 Tips to "Having It All," and getting the "Best for Less" what does it mean to "Get *R.E.A.L.* with yourself? Most of you may be saying, "But Di$count Diva, I am real," and you may be, but are you "*R.E.A.L.*" with yourself? So just what is *R.E.A.L.*? *R.E.A.L.* is an acronym that stands for *R*ealistic *E*xpectations *A*bout *L*ife. Now the question remains, are you realistic in your expectations about what you need, desire, and can afford, and are these expectations based on your current station in life? Here are some questions you should ask yourself to see if you have *R*ealistic *E*xpectations *A*bout *L*ife.

1. Are you driving a car that you cannot afford, thus you sigh about your payments or cringe when it's time to get something fixed? This also includes paying for tags, maintenance and repairs, gas, and insurance.
2. Do you go on a shopping spree when you only have little to no money in the bank? This means you really can't afford the spree, but you're more focused on taking care of your wants versus your needs.
3. Do you often buy things you can't afford in order to keep up appearances, go on trips you can't afford, or go out for drinks with girlfriends when it's not in your budget? This

includes financing things on credit or spending a substantial amount of money on "trinkets" because you think you should have or deserve these things.

4. Do you try to help family members and friends who ask for money when you can barely pay your own bills? This means you really shouldn't be helping others, but you're too scared to tell them "No!"

5. Are you up late nights wondering how you can afford your lifestyle and achieve your dreams? This means you can't sleep because you are overspending and are worried you won't be able to afford the home, dream vacation, or business you want.

If you answered "Yes" to three out of five questions, you do NOT have *R*ealistic *E*xpectations *A*bout *L*ife. The good thing is that there is help for you! You can develop realistic expectations by changing a few of your habits and checking yourself. For example, get real with yourself by figuring out what you want for your life. How much money does it take for you to live the lifestyle you want to live? What is your passion, and what kind of jobs will allow you to work in your area of passion and make an income comfortable for yourself? In other words, your passion may be teaching, which is wonderful; however, if the teaching income is $40,000/year, it is highly unlikely you will be able to afford a $300,000 home. Does this mean you should not follow your passion to teach? Of course not, you should teach, **BUT** you should also find a way to make some additional income so you can purchase the home you want.

You might start a home-based business, or tutor on the side, or continue in your professional development so you can become a specialist or administrator and therefore increase your income potential. Whatever the case, you must have a plan and you must be *realistic* about what you want in your life.

Getting "R.E.A.L" with yourself means establishing where you are in life, where you are going, and where you want to be. A sure-fire way to develop *R*ealistic *E*xpectations *A*bout *L*ife is through developing financial goals. Just as you create goals for everything else, it is important to create goals about your finances. Be sure when developing goals that you relate them to what is important to you, e.g., relationships, health, family. Goals should be easily measurable and you should allot yourself a reasonable amount of time to achieve them.

When establishing goals you should develop short, intermediate, and long-term goals. Short-term goals would be those you accomplish in zero to six months, intermediate in six months to one year, and long-term in more than a year. In putting this in financial terms, a short-term goal for someone who answered "Yes" to three of the above questions could be "I want to refinance my car for a lower rate or sell it and get a less expensive car within six months." An intermediate goal could be "I want to take a vacation within the next year and not go broke," and a long-term goal could be "I want to purchase a home and be able to afford a down payment and closing costs within five years."

Now, in having *R*ealistic *E*xpectations *A*bout *L*ife, it is important to develop a plan to attain your goals. For instance, will you need to shift some of your spending around to be able to comfortably afford the home you want? How much will you need to save to be able to take that dream vacation? Are there things you need to cut out to achieve your goals, like daily coffee runs, eating out excessively, or shopping whenever you get a whim? What is it going to actually take to get you the things you want in your life? If you can't be *real* with me, at least be *real* with yourself.

Now that we've dealt with the financial side, let's look at the personal side. At some point, you have to ask yourself, "Why am I doing these things? Whom am I trying to impress? Do these things make me who I am?" The answer to the last question should be a resounding, "No!" If it's not, then you have some work to do. It's not just about getting *R.E.A.L.* in your finances, it's about getting *R.E.A.L.* in your life! Remember, it's *R*ealistic *E*xpectations *A*bout *L*ife, and if you are making these kinds of decisions it is time to do some soul searching as to why you are making them.

Did you grow up in a situation where impressing people meant buying things that were high end, even if you couldn't afford them? Living like this will always put you at a disadvantage. You will always be in the hole, and you will never be able to get out because there will always be another high-end product that comes out that you want to buy. While you are going around trying to impress other people, most of the time they aren't even paying you any attention, and out of those who are, many don't even like you. It's like paying for a big wedding when you can only afford a small ceremony. Why would you pay tens of thousands of dollars to feed people who are going to talk about whether you have a wedding Donald Trump style or Donald Duck style? It doesn't make sense and neither does spending money to impress people.

Were you so in need of approval that you were willing to buy things you couldn't afford just to be a part of the "in crowd"? Well, I'll tell you what. I don't want to be a part of the "in crowd." The "in crowd" will get you in trouble and have you broke. The people who are the wealthiest, most awe-inspiring people in this world often went against the crowd, from The Messiah to Bill Gates, who dropped out of college. The crowd says, "Go to school, get a good education, so you can get a good job" -- and Bill Gates quit school. So now is he a quitter or a winner? You decide, but going with the "in crowd" has never been a way to achieve success and that's what we're all trying to do here, be a success. Now, I'm not telling you to drop out of school or that your degree is worthless, but I am telling you not to be so focused on doing what the crowd says is right. Be focused on what *you* say is right!

Do you have fear of rejection? Are you afraid if you don't go to an event, or if you re-prioritize your life around your dreams, goals, aspirations, and what's financially appropriate for you, then you will lose friends? This to me is the worst kind of thinking of them all, because if your friendships ride on whether or not you can spend money to hang out with friends, then they're not *real* friends. This may be a bitter pill to swallow, but if you can't hang out with your friends when you are broke or when you don't want to spend money or when you are working toward other financial goals, then that's a problem. Then the question remains, is it that they don't want to hang out with you or you don't want to hang out with them? Sometimes, we don't want to hang out with our friends when our money is not right. We feel embarrassed or ashamed, so we spend money we can't afford to because we don't want people to know our *real* status, as if when they know they will say, "Uggghhh, you're broke." Either you are shallow or your friends are, but it needs to be fixed!

Then maybe you're just immature and you like to have fun at any cost. I must admit, I'm just getting free of this myself. My nature is I am a social butterfly. I love, love, love to have fun. I'm adventurous and I love to entertain. I also like to take care of those I love by giving gifts. For example, in the past, if I was out shopping and saw a cute pair of shoes in a size 5 ½ and they were super cheap, I would just pick them up for my friend who wears that size. No expectation of her to pay me for them. I just love her and wanted to get her those cute shoes.

I would plan parties, teas, and events at my home just because I like to entertain. Even if I hadn't budgeted for it, I would just pull the money from somewhere else. But eventually I decided I had other, more important obligations to fulfill, like building my business. Instead of concentrating on attending a party, I decided to concentrate on doing what was really important, and that is building my life. I had a gut check when I planned to attend a weekend getaway that I hadn't budgeted for and was gonna spend money I didn't need to spend, but then got an awesome business opportunity that same weekend. After getting over my initial nausea, I decided to be an adult and make a mature, slightly painful (only to my inner party girl) yet lucrative decision. I haven't looked back since.

You see, everything I have taught in this book, I have lived. I'm not saying I know it all or have all the answers. I'm not a trained financial advisor and I don't hold certifications, but what I do hold is a Ph.D. in learning how to "Have It All for Less." I learned the less you spend and more you keep, the easier and quicker you can build wealth and really *Have It All,* and I hope this book gets you off to a great start!

So establish a plan of action, and begin decisively taking steps toward achieving that plan. Then you can say you have gotten, *R.E.A.L.* with yourself, and you will be well on your way to "Having It All" in every area of your life.

ABOUT THE AUTHOR

Lynesha McElveen, known as The Di$count Diva™, is the owner of Liberty Educational Group (L.E.G.) and L.E.G.acy Builders.

She has a passion for working with people of all ages and educating them about their life, finances, and health.

Her work with L.E.G. gives her the opportunity to coach people on attaining financial freedom, walking in greatness, and increasing their personal potential.

She promotes health and wellness through educating girls and women in caring for their spirit, soul, and body and by helping them develop self-esteem, sound character, and discipline. Lynesha mentors and encourages others to follow their dreams and build a lasting legacy.

Lynesha has worked with major universities including Georgia State University, Spelman College, and Clark Atlanta University. She has also worked with Habitat for Humanity, Watch Her Work/Bad Boy Entertainment, Ready to Launch, and the Police Athletic League teaching financial principles, entrepreneurship, and personal development. Featured in Black Enterprise and interviewed by the Urban Business Roundtable and Views from the Top, she is a sought after expert.

Lynesha has written for Empower Me! Magazine and is a monthly contributor to Hope for Women Magazine. Now partnering with Operation Hope and Junior Achievement, Lynesha hopes to continue improving the world around her by educating, empowering and serving others… one day at a time.

For additional information, please visit:
www.LyneshaMcelveen.com